The Way
Is
Within

IRIS -

BE

AND ALL WILL BE

Love
your friend

Rod

The Way
Is
Within

A Spiritual Journey

Ron Rathbun

BERKLEY BOOKS, NEW YORK

THE WAY IS WITHIN

A Berkley Book / published by arrangement with
the author

PRINTING HISTORY
Quiescence Publishing edition / October 1994
Berkley trade paperback edition / January 1997

The Penguin Putnam Inc. World Wide Web site address is
http://www.penguinputnam.com

ISBN: 0-425-15460-2

BERKLEY®
Berkley Books are published by The Berkley Publishing Group,
a division of Penguin Putnam Inc.,
375 Hudson Street, New York, New York 10014.
BERKLEY and the "B" design
are trademarks belonging to Penguin Putnam Inc.

PRINTED IN THE UNITED STATES OF AMERICA

10   9   8   7   6   5

Acknowledgments

There are many people I want to thank for helping with this labor of love.

My wife, Lavana—without her help, this book might not have been written.

Gene, my teacher and friend, for showing me the value of meditation.

Paul Riha, a special thank-you with heart-felt appreciation for layout, typography and book design.

Sheri Wachtstetter for her watercolor paintings on the chapter title pages.

For editing and review:
Dave Harvey, Terrea McCoy, Kathy Miller, Jill Grassie, Dan Conway, Maureen Brown and Claudia Riha for final editing and proofing.

*"This is a spiritual journey
from the outside world
to a place beyond words
that only you
can find within."*

Contents

"*As truly and completely
as it can be said,
the
Way Is Within.*"

The Beginning

This story begins many years ago at the age of nineteen. I was a troubled youth, as almost all teenagers are; I was rebelling and trying to fit in at the same time. Neither was working. All of my peers were into things outside themselves; who had this and who had that. Many of them were trying to impress others with what they had. The feeling of competing for things outside myself left me empty inside. I would watch people pretending to be someone other than who they were. It all seemed so shallow. I found myself leaving my peers and wanting to be alone more and more. I was looking for answers to painful situations.

One lonely night I cried out to the universe, "Is this all there is?" A short time later I had what could be called a waking dream. I saw three Chinese men dressed in green robes in front of me. I thought to myself, "Is this really happening?" I had never experienced anything like this before. Curious as I am, I asked, "Who are you?" To my surprise they said, "We are friends and have come to teach you." Keep in mind, at this time I still thought this was some sort of dream. They asked me to come study with them. I wondered to myself, "Why me?" They said, "Come with us." I asked, "How can this be done?" They said,

"Quiet your mind and we will take you." So I quieted my mind and a feeling came over me that I cannot explain and from that moment on I knew my life was going to be changed somehow. I felt a sensation of movement but could not tell where I was going. I had no fear, so I just relaxed. When the movement stopped I found myself in a dark hallway. I wondered where I was. The whole experience was like a dream but not like a dream because it felt different. I walked down the hallway and in a doorway to the left was a library with scrolls and written works of many different kinds. I went over to what looked like a window. Through the window I could see huge mountains in the background that looked like the Himalayas. I thought to myself, "Where is this place?" All of a sudden one of the men in green robes appeared. He said I could come here and study any time, if I so choose, by just quieting my mind and visualizing this place. He bowed to me and the experience was over.

I wondered about the experience in the back of my mind for some time. Somehow there was something different about the images I had seen, so I began to practice to see if I indeed could go back to this mysterious place. As I practiced visualizing, I began to see more clearly. What I saw was a monastery that sat at the edge of a large cliff with the Himalayas in the background and a valley below.

The monastery itself was a simple place, made mostly of rock and stone with a few windows here and there. There were candles in the hallways to light your way, but for the most part it was dimly lit. Facing west and to the right was a large room for meetings. Down the main hallway and to the left was the library. There was a window on the east wall of the library which had no glass and yet the wind did not seem to blow through. There were scrolls in cubby holes on two walls and in the middle of the floor, a low table to spread them out and read them. Sometimes while in the library I saw other people but they mostly kept to themselves. Although I saw relatively few people there, the people I saw were from all nationalities. Race, creed or color of skin did not matter here.

One day when I was in the library a priest entered who I had not seen before. He was interesting; he was very old looking but seemed very young at the same time. He told me I had reached the age of internment and to follow him. I followed him down a stairway to another level below. We walked down a hallway with a line of doors until we reached the fifth door on the right, where he stopped. He opened the door and said, "This is your room. You may come here any time you wish."

This room was quite small and starkly furnished, but filled with a feeling of great warmth. While in my room, if I needed help with something all I had to do was think about help and a teacher would just seem to appear, talk for awhile and as quickly as he came he would be gone. The priests' minds were so clear they just knew when I was looking for help. From time to time each of the three teachers, who told me they were Tibetan Buddhist priests, would show me scrolls and translate them into English for me. After the experience I would come back and write down the passages as soon as possible. I began to understand that this was not a dream but something different. I kept what I was doing to myself for many years because of what others might think. I just continued to collect knowledge and enjoy what I was doing.

Over a period of many years I have gone to this little room. The conversations between myself and the priests were about many things. Many times while these conversations were happening I would be thinking to myself, "The world needs to be hearing these things. There are so many problems in the world and these people have so many answers, answers that are simple and easy to understand."

I now know that spirituality is not of dreams but a place of beauty and reality within that we can all choose to have. I look forward to every time I quiet my mind and go within because of the incredible beauty and understanding that I have found inside myself. Once you sense beauty on this level, it will change your life forever.

Go slow in reading this book and ponder the beauty and understanding of the words. The words in italics are direct quotes from my teachers. In regular print are discussions between the priests and myself about the quotes. The depth of your understanding of these words will be in direct proportion to the understanding you have about yourself. Some of these teachings are so seemingly easy to understand that the deeper meaning is often lost. I find the teachings to be the golden thread of truth that runs throughout all cultures and all walks of life. All of the words have been said many times before, but it is only when you take the time in self-study that you will truly understand the hidden meaning in these messages. If you do not understand something right away, give your mind time to put into place the knowledge and wisdom.

As your spiritual growth and awareness deepen, so will your understanding about truth. Truth is ever-changing, timeless and yet always the same. Learn to calm your mind and when the time is right, the door will open; such is the way. If there is a common denominator in what all of these teachers have said, it is to slow down, go within and enjoy your life. Fill your mind with beauty, love and understanding and you will become it.

This spiritual journey has been a labor of love spanning eighteen years of intense study with some of the wisest and most beautiful people I have ever met. What I have found through my spiritual journey is that there is much more to life than just what is in the outside world. There is a world within that has beauty beyond belief. Beauty on this level, is what I hope all people will experience in their life and the reason I have written this book.

"*The grass is always greener on the other side because that is where you are looking. Look to this side, not the other side. This side is now. The other side is tomorrow.*"

Chapter One
Images of the Mind

WACHSTETTER

*The picture you create in your mind
is the picture you live in.
Go slow,
a great masterpiece is not hurried!
You have as much time as you allow yourself.
Notice the detail in your picture
and when something does not feel right,
stop,
stand back and ask, "Why?"
Is the picture of your life a masterpiece
or something indistinguishable?*

You are the painter of your life. Learn to paint in detail so the picture of your life will have clarity. Often it is the attention to detail that is very important and can make the difference between something haphazard and something of great purpose.

There may be many times when you do not feel comfortable about your direction in life. This is an opportunity to stop and give yourself some time to gain focus. This pause can make the difference between an accomplishment and a mistake. We all make mistakes, but the biggest mistake is to not learn from them.

When something in your life does not feel comfortable, STOP, stand back and ask, "Why?" This is a very powerful and profound tool!

Your mind is a place you can go to anytime.
Within it is everything you seek.
Your expression of how you feel
comes from it.
Should you not take care of your mind
so that the expression is of the highest order?

Within your mind is every emotion and thought that you can possibly imagine. Each emotion and thought produces a certain feeling inside yourself.

Which emotions and thoughts do you choose to have in your life?

You are the only one who can decide which emotions and thoughts are for your highest and best good.

Your mind is like a double-edged sword. The edge of beauty moves with grace and appreciation while the edge of ugliness cuts with ignorance and disdain. Your mind can create beauty or ugliness. Watch carefully, in your mind, how the emotions of beauty and ugliness differ.

Which emotion is comfortable and which is not?

Which edge of your mind do you use most often, beauty or ugliness?

Your mind is the most powerful tool there is; learn to keep it sharp and in your control.

*Your mind
works in many ways.
Do you know in what ways?*

Find out how to use your mind, what brings harmony to your life and what does not. Empty your mind of thoughts each day and it will be easier to see your problems.

Many of the problems in life are people-related. People interfering in the lives of others. When people do things you don't like and it affects you, it is your problem, not theirs. These problems manifest as negative buttons inside of you that others can push, with or without your knowing it.

Find the buttons in your mind that make you lose control and learn to disconnect them. Ensure that no one controls you, but you. It is you who must be aware of your buttons and work to remove them through contemplation. They will not disappear on their own without work on your part! The moment you find someone pushing one of your buttons ask yourself, "Why is this happening?" This is the question that leads to the answer.

Do not let anyone control you. Set yourself free by getting rid of your buttons. It is awareness and control from within which bring us fulfillment. CONTROL YOURSELF—not others. Let others be who they are and you will free yourself from them. Release yourself from karma (cause and effect) by allowing people to be who they are.

When you have released yourself from your own buttons and you have released everyone else by allowing them to be who they are, you will have gained great freedom.

Stand
in your own space
and know
you are there.

The space you stand in is you. Center yourself in your own space at all times.

If you do not know where you stand within yourself, where does that leave you?

Your space can be interrupted by many things and only you can decide whether or not to allow interruptions into your space.

The interruptions you create inside yourself will be the most challenging of your life because you cannot walk away from them. Just as there are interruptions within, there are interruptions without. Both interruptions will require work on your part to rid them from your space.

Learning to control your mind will teach you how to allow some things in and how to allow other things to pass by.

Your space, without mental control, can be a prison without a key. The key is controlling your mind. Learn to control your mind, then your space can be any beautiful place. It is your choice.

How many times will you hear, "It is your choice," before you understand, you truly choose?

When you stand centered in your own space and know you are there, it will become clear what your choices are and which ones to make.

It is not bad
that you would have a conversation
with yourself.
It is however,
when you know not who's talking.

If there is too much chatter in your mind it is hard to tell where your thoughts are coming from. From learning to gain control of your mind will come clear thinking. From clear thinking will come the difference between constructive and destructive thoughts.

Constructive thoughts are never the problem. Problems come from destructive, uncontrolled thoughts.

If you never take time to train your mind, how can you control it?

Most problems in life are fear based. Remember, there is nothing that can possess you against your will. The only demons are the ones you have created in your own mind because of fear. Do not try to block out fear, confront it and learn why it is there. End the destructive cycle of fear and worry by understanding where it comes from. Take time to find out who you are so that you do not scare yourself with your own thoughts.

Try this exercise: sit down, get comfortable and literally watch the thoughts that cross your mind. Keep a journal to record your thoughts. Your recorded thoughts will be a mirror image of yourself.

After doing this exercise for a period of time you will know who is talking. It will be you.

*W*here your mind is,
is where you are.

Where are your thoughts during the day?

Take some time to watch your mind and see what it thinks.

Are you where your thoughts are?

If you are not where your thoughts are, it is easy to feel out-of-sync with yourself. Scattered thoughts can leave you with a feeling of being neither here nor there. If this happens, slow down and calm your mind so that your thoughts of where you are and what you are doing are the same.

It is unmindful and difficult for your mind to be in two places at once.

If you are working—work.

If you are playing—play.

There is only one moment in time, the one you are in right now!

The true meaning of being MINDFUL is experienced when you are living in the moment and enjoying it.

*You are
what you think
you are!
What do you think
you are?*

What do you think you are?

This is one of the most profound questions you can ask yourself.

The answer to this question defines who you are.

You create your thoughts and your thoughts create your life. Do you like what you have created?

If you do not know how to change the way you think, how can you change your life?

How do you bring spiritual change into your life?

By simplifying your life, by slowing down your thought process and taking time for introspection.

In changing the way you think, you change your world.

Contemplate yourself each day and you will unravel the mystery of not only what you are but who you are.

Do not get caught up in old patterns,
things that do not work,
do not work!
Change!
Your attitude adjusts your abilities.

We all have patterns by which we operate in our lives: the way we see things, the way we do things, the way we live. Do our patterns work?

Are you comfortable in how your life works or do you need to change the way you do things?

Use the abilities within your mind to break ineffective or destructive patterns. Have a spiritual attitude in what you do and you will create harmonious results in your life.

There is one sure method of identifying spiritual truths in your life. THEY WORK! Spiritual truth is not something outside you; it is within you in your understanding of life. All spiritual truths in life will set you free. If the truth does not set you free, it is not the truth, it is dogma! Dogma is created from the inability of an individual to see the truth. The real truth in life is found in the hearts and minds of all who sincerely seek it within.

If a truth is complex, PAY ATTENTION because this is a sure sign something is not right!

Spiritual truths are simple, simply because they work that way!

A bowl of rice filled is good!
A mind filled is better.
A mind filled with disharmony
is not filled, but empty.
A glass upside down
can gather no water.
So the mind cannot quench its thirst
when it is in disharmony.
When the physical needs are met,
what lies ahead,
emptiness or fullness?

It is important and appropriate to take care of your physical needs, but when that is done what is next?

Learn to take care of your mind as well as your body. If you do not give your body proper attention it breaks down. So it is with your mind. When your mind is in disharmony it is hard to feel good about anything.

Think of your mind as an empty glass. When it is empty it can be filled with knowledge and awareness. From an empty mind will come both the seen and the unseen. Between hard, coarse, analytical thoughts and soft, subtle, spiritual thoughts is the knowledge and wisdom of all time. Drink of the knowledge and wisdom within you when you are truly thirsty for life. It is a bottomless well within you. The only time your well will be empty is when you cannot find it.

One day all will understand beyond words why emptiness in the mind is fullness.

The clouds on the horizon
are a warning of things to come.
A warning is not necessarily associated
with ugliness or negative actions.
You make the choice
on what to warn yourself about.
A warning is neither negative nor positive,
but of something to come.
The question is, "Do you want it to come?"
How can it be negative or positive
if you choose to experience it?
It is one experience
in a string of lifetime experiences.

As your mind starts slowing down its thought process and you become more sensitive, you will begin to sense things before they happen. There is no mystery in this. You have merely opened a part of your mind to a higher kind of awareness.

Sensing things before they happen is a natural by-product of a quiet mind. There is a saying, "Fore warned is fore armed." When you sense something before it happens, you have a choice to step around it or experience it. The best possible defense is to avoid the wrong place at the wrong time.

All the tools and abilities within the mind are there to use. But you must first find them in the subtler levels within your mind. There are many kinds of tools, from a gut-level feeling to a knowing which cannot be explained. But remember, the most powerful tool of all is the one you control. When you can control the subtle forces of your mind, you will have found an incredible ally.

Life
is the meaning
we make it.

How is it that such a small statement can have such profound meaning?

It is from the control of our minds that the meaning of life becomes understood, from the outward existence of the physical to the inward comprehension of absolute mind.

How is it that meaning is given to your life?

Where does meaning in your life come from?

The meaning of your life can be anything from simple thoughts to analytical thinking, the theory of a philosophy, to the deeper more subtle levels that go beyond what can be said in words.

In many ways your mind is like a crystal ball. If you do not polish it daily it becomes dull and so will your senses. When your senses become dull, so will your life. Awaken your senses and they will bring you out of the deep sleep of laziness into the true meaning of life, with only one catch. You are the only one who can wake yourself up. Polishing your mind requires investing time into understanding yourself.

Within you is the knowledge and understanding of every great sage and wise teacher. Still your mind and you will recognize the teacher. It is you.

"*The spiritual pathway*
can take many directions
and not all of them fruitful.
Remember,
each is a lesson.
A lesson of learning
about ourselves."

Seeking Your Pathway

*Your pathway is your own,
so make it a good one,
a pathway where others
will be glad to walk with you.*

If you want someone to walk with you on your pathway through life, it is wise to know who you are and where you are going. If you are in the dark about who you are and what you want, you and the person you seek may pass right by each other and not even know it. From knowing who you are, it is easier to find someone who seeks the same things as you.

Attract whom you want in your life by the thoughts you think, rather than mere chance. Think beautiful thoughts and you will attract beauty.

There is a law in the universe known as: LIKE ATTRACTS LIKE. You attract people who are most like you.

Within each one of us is a perception most people do not use, the ability to sense with your mind, known to many as a gut-level feeling. Use this sense to know how and where to find friends. Ask yourself, "What do I feel about this or that person?" Practice sensing with your mind. You will be surprised by what the mind can do.

When you know more about who you are, you will know more about who you want to walk with you.

*T*ry to see each step of your path,
not as a trail to follow,
but as a way to live.

Many people follow a philosophy or religion blindly because of what is expected and they forget to live their own lives.

Everyone's life is a pathway to perfection, but not everyone takes the same path. If the path you are on does not feel comfortable, it may not be the right path. Only you can decide what is right or wrong in your life. It is your life to live. Learn to see, hear, touch and feel with all your senses and know for yourself what life is about.

All the spiritual knowledge which exists in the world exists within you, not in something outside you. There are no historical writings or spiritual laws that are sacred, IT IS THE EXPERIENCE OF LIFE THAT IS SACRED.

How can any lifeless thing be more sacred than that which is living?

How can it be any other way? It can never be!

All true spiritual laws are laws because not following them produces disharmony. If you do not live in accordance with the natural laws of the universe, you will simply suffer. The suffering comes, not as a punishment, but from not using your mind to see the truth about what you are doing in your life.

Everyone, at some point in their life, looks for the right pathway or trail to follow. Always remember, your pathway is within you, not outside you.

*F*ollow not others in your life.
Follow your heart
and each day will be yours,
not somebody else's.

Feel with your heart and you will find it. Follow your heart and it will lead you.

The confusion in people comes in following others' lives, not their own. Do what feels right in your heart and you will know it is right. Live your life your way, not the way of others. If you are following someone else's life, you are going their direction, not yours.

Everyone is going to the same place, but not everyone takes the same path to get there. We will all learn the same basic things in life, but we may not learn them at the same time.

When seeking a spiritual teacher, know that true spiritual teachers lead people back within themselves. A true spiritual teacher does not try to make people conform to a philosophy but shows them the pathway to find the harmony within.

If your spiritual intentions are in a belief system outside you—be careful. One sure way to know if your spiritual intentions and your pathway are the same is that they will be in harmony.

Your spiritual pathway does not come from following others but from soul searching your life.

Is this not the true pathway?

There are those
who would follow the easy way,
that of following someone outside themselves.
If you are following a sheep herder,
you do not understand
that you are your own sheep herder.
A flock is not lead but guarded,
guarded against the interference of others.
It is a wise man that points out this difference.

Everyone, on some level, knows what direction is the right direction to go in life. Your heart and mind already know all the answers. Learn to clear your mind and you will see and understand what those answers are. Just as no one can give you well-being, no one can give you what you already possess within. We must all learn for ourselves what we are about and what our life means to us.

How can anyone know yourself more than you?

Nobody in all reality can lead your life for you, because they are not you. If you are living in the shadow of another, you are not living in your own true light.

Stand in your own light from within. It is your spiritual right, because it is your life.

Walking softly
will not only
make your pathway easier,
but more quiet too.

There is enough confusion in the world without bothering others with unnecessary noise and lack of awareness.

A wise man always walks slowly and softly.

Do you know why?

When you walk slowly and softly you have time to appreciate and hear where you are going. While walking quietly it is easier to hear yourself think in a world full of noise and confusion.

Try this exercise: go out for a walk. As you walk become aware of your pace. Find a pace which feels comfortable to you. Then, look at the beauty of the world around you and feel your place in it. Now, combine walking while feeling a oneness with your surroundings. You will sense a very interesting thing—truly walking a spiritual pathway through life!

Look at your feet.
If you do not like
where you are standing,
MOVE!

Standing in a place where you are not comfortable is unwise, and yet people have a tendency to get into habitual patterns of doing the same thing, day after day whether they like it or not. This is not living, but a poor existence.

Many times people stay in places they don't like because they are afraid to move. Staying in the same place because of fear and apprehension is like living on a hamster wheel. Step off the hamster wheel by flowing with the changes in your life. Be it a mental or physical change, flow with it.

When you do not know what direction to move in life, move slowly. Moving slowly is the mark of a wise man. While moving slowly you have the opportunity to see things in detail, things you may have missed while going too fast.

If you do not like where you are in your life, move!

It really is as simple as that!

Change
is something we must all deal with.
Are you changing it
or is it changing you?
Where lies the control of change?

CHANGE IS THE ONLY CONSTANT IN THE UNIVERSE and also a spiritual and physical law in play at all times.

There is no way to avoid change. We are on the pathway of change whether we like it or not. If you work and flow with change, you will learn and grow to be patient.

If you resist change, you will struggle against the flow of life itself. The struggle then becomes frustration which becomes your constant companion.

Which companion do you choose to walk with, patience or frustration?

Where lies the control of change?

There is only one answer, as there is only one person change affects: YOU.

Change happens to everyone but affects only you and how you deal with it.

Are you hard and rigid, set in your ways?

Or are you growing wiser and more graceful with each day?

*It is only when you see
what you are doing
is of no value,
that it really is.*

Many times as we walk along our spiritual pathway we do not take the time to see the value in what we do. It is from a sense of value that we receive a deeper meaning in everything in our life.

How much of each moment in each day do you value your life?

If you do not have a sense of value, will you have a sense of appreciation?

There are small steps or accomplishments on your pathway all the time, but because they are not big, important steps, many times we do not value them. This is wrong thinking! All steps, accomplishments or spiritual progress of any kind are of value.

Is not a small step better than no step at all?

Is it not by the small steps that we get to the big steps?

And do you really know that the small step is not actually a big step?

As you delve deeper into the experience within your mind you will find subtlety is understanding often overlooked. Many times it is the small, subtle steps that are really the significant ones.

When you find thoughts and feelings within your mind that are hard to put into words—PAY ATTENTION. You have found something quite valuable.

To see things as they really are,
to walk a pathway as it really is,
and use the two together,
is wisdom,
the way it really is.

We are all involved in the dance of life.

Those who know the dance, dance well and enjoy it. Those who know not the dance often stumble. If you cannot see the dance of life for what it is, it may not be a dance at all, but something disliked.

Your pathway can be a dance, a walk or a run. However you choose to move through life, think carefully before you make decisions. Think about what you do before you do it. A wise man's pathway happens in individual steps—you observe, you contemplate, you understand and then you do.

Seeing things the way they really are will lead you to a profound truth. Things are the way they are, simply because it is the natural order of things in the universe.

Learn to see things the way they really are and you will find yourself becoming less and less surprised and more and more content.

*Place in your own hands
your destiny,
then you will not be
at the mercy of others.*

If your destiny is in the hands of others, so is the control of your life.

Watch carefully the direction of your life.

From your own mind will come your own destiny.

Learn to see for yourself so you will not be at the mercy of others. Not everyone may be as merciful as you. You are the only person who can give yourself the destiny you desire. Allowing your destiny to be controlled by someone else is a lack of understanding.

We are all heading towards our own destiny and understanding yourself is the pathway to that destiny.

Your life can be a game of fun and adventure when controlled by you or a game of fear and chance when controlled by another.

It is important to know the rules of a game or the game can be a mystery.

Is the game you play in life one of more mystery or more understanding?

"You are holding
the key to your inner-self;
get comfortable
with holding the key.
The key
is inner-knowing.
And yes,
you are the only one
holding the key."

Chapter Three

Finding Your Inner-Self

WACHSTETTER

It is a wise man that listens to his inner-self.
The outside world can be a beautiful place.
But without knowledge of the inside world
one is often lost,
aimlessly wandering,
looking to a world with very few answers,
when standing at one's feet
is the answer.

If you are only aware of the outside world, you are only living a part of your life. If you take time to quiet your mind every day, you will learn to hear your inner-self.

The world inside you is as real as the outside world, but because it is harder to see, hear and understand, many people do not take the time to learn from it.

Your inside world determines what your outside world will look like. Should you not pay attention to it?

Learn to quiet your mind to see your inner world or it may not exist.

There are many states of mind within you—fear, worry, sadness—or if you choose—love, happiness, well-being. Where are you?

Listen to your inner-self and you will see your world within. If you do not take the time to look within, you may very well find yourself aimlessly wandering.

*Promise yourself
to be you.
It will be
the most important promise
you will ever make.*

Who else can you be, other than who you are?

You could try to be someone else to please others but you would not be you. You would be who someone wants you to be.

Do not change your life for another person; it will always be for the wrong reason. At some point in time you will resent the change because it was not your decision to change. No one likes to be told what to do against their wishes. If your decision to change was your own, you would not need to be told. You would just do it!

Everyone knows from within what is right and what is wrong. Do what is right and be yourself!

Be who you are and you will see it is the most important promise you will ever make.

*T*he true expression
of life
is a clear expression
of you.

The expression of who you are inside and who you are outside are not always the same. It is who you are inside that is the real expression of you.

Do not be afraid to be who you are because of what others might think. If someone cannot see and appreciate your beauty, they are not worthy of it.

Find in yourself your likes and dislikes. From your likes and dislikes comes the knowledge of what your expression is.

What do you appreciate and why?

What do you dislike and why?

From your likes and dislikes come feelings. These feelings are signposts along your pathway that can tell you many things about your expression of life.

Are your signs taking you the direction you want to go?

*A peach blossom
is what it is.
I would suggest
you do the same.*

All living creatures and things of nature are what they are, with the exception of mankind.

We are the only creatures who can be something other than who we are. We can pretend that we are someone or something else or we can choose to see the way we really are. This is a fine line for many people, yet defines the difference between delusion and reality.

Be very careful when you are someone different than who you really are. This is delusion!

How much of the time are you who you really are?

And when you are not yourself, who are you?

Learn to be who you are.

In a complex world of many people, places and things to do it is easy to get distracted. Take time each day to center and feel who you are so you do not become lost in a world of complexity and confusion.

When we all find who we are, we will find our place in nature and in life.

Then we will be like the peach blossom.

The only thing we can be, who we are, ourselves.

*Look within
and find
what you are not about!
What have you not done
that you need to?*

Look at what you are doing in your life, or in this case, look the opposite direction at what you are not doing.

What have you not done that you need to?

Do you feel somehow something is missing in your life?

Do you have trouble understanding your life and the way things are?

There is a reason for all things if you look diligently.

From what you do not understand about yourself will come the understanding of who you are and your relationship with the world. In essence, YOU are what you are looking for. Within your essence is everything.

How is it that the essence of your being is often overlooked?

For many people their essence is a mystery and clouded by their hopes and desires of attaining things other than their true essence.

How do you find what you do not know is missing? By becoming aware of what your essence is.

The writing is on the wall.
It just depends
on what wall you are looking at.
Everything is already there.
Center yourself in that.
That,
that is you!

We are all here to read and understand what is written within our soul. Written within you is everything you need to know.

Should you not look within often?

It is fine to admire what another has written on the wall of his mind, but remember, your life is written on your wall, not someone else's. Each one of us is unique and our lives written a little differently. Make your writing beautiful so you are pleased with what you have written.

Everything in the world means nothing if you cannot read your own writing. Remember, all the knowledge to read, write and learn is already written within you.

*The study of one's self
can be a profound experience.
It can of course
because of you.
What is required of you
is study.*

The study of yourself should be the most profound experience of your life. It is what you are here to do.

Open your mind and you will discover amazing things. You will discover who you are.

The pathway toward enlightenment is a singular pathway, as must be your studies. The teacher can only point the way; it is the student who must walk the pathway.

If you are to learn spiritual awareness you must learn patience. This is very important. Patience will give you the time to do your studies. From your studies will come the awareness of yourself and the pathway you walk. What is required of you is study—MEDITATION (stilling the mind), INTROSPECTION and CONTEMPLATION. This is the path of inner-knowing.

Make your life a profound experience by taking time for self-study. The rewards will be as great or as little as what you give to yourself.

*Make friends
with yourself
and you will have friends.*

Friends will come and friends will go, but you, you can never walk away from yourself.

For what reason would you not be your own best friend?

From the knowledge within, you will discover who your best friend is—yourself. Make friends with yourself and you will have a friend.

If you are not a friend to yourself, how can you be a friend to anyone else?

When you are in times of trouble and do not feel like being a friend to yourself, do not take out your anger or frustration on others. Take time to be alone until you calm down and can see more clearly. Emotional problems are flags saying—pay attention—you have something to learn here. Our problems give us the opportunity to learn and grow. Give yourself some time to work out your problems.

BE KIND TO YOURSELF. This is a profound statement!

Let not times of trial weigh you down. You are always worth far more than you know.

Find love, respect and trust within and you will build a foundation upon which friendships will last a lifetime.

It is the common man
who sees who he is,
because he is not trying to be
who he is not.
Be in common with yourself,
not with others.
The common goal of man
is to be one with himself.

If you try to please others by being someone else, you are playing a game. Be careful not to play too long, lest you forget you are playing and the game becomes trouble—delusion.

Be very careful of delusion; it occurs when you cannot see things for what they really are. Delusion is a maze that only leads to a nightmare.

When you cannot find your way and you are lost, find your way in the thought that you are love, even when you cannot feel it for yourself. Time will draw you into love like a moth to a flame. The flame is the light of awareness from within.

Be who you are and you will see yourself in your own true light. Anything that is not seen in its true light is in some form of darkness.

When you are in common with yourself, you are in common with what all people look for in their life, themselves.

Wearing the clothes
does not make the man.
Knowing the man,
makes the man.
Know yourself
and then wear what you like.

The robes of a monk are simple because his mind is simple. He need not express what is of little importance to him.

How beautiful the world would be if the glow of awareness and beauty from within overshadowed people's physical clothing. The physical clothing you put on will wear out with time but your spiritual clothing will only become stronger and more beautiful with each use.

Dress your inner-self with beautiful thoughts each day and you will be dressed for any occasion. Shopping from a storehouse of enlightenment within your mind is a store beyond belief with everything you could ever want or dream of.

Are you more beautifully dressed on the inside or the outside of yourself?

What price can you put on knowing what is within you?

*When you have worth
exceeding your physical worth,
you are truly rich.*

The true measure of a rich person is inner wealth, not material gain.

A wise man once said, "Where your heart is, there also will you find your treasure."

Your world within is who you really are. Spend more time inside and the rewards will be as tangible as any physical worth outside.

Spiritual well-being and physical well-being are yours to have but far too often people serve only one master, money or the illusion of well-being that comes from it.

Everyone is looking for a sense of well-being but many people do not know where to look. Look within; all the well-being in the world is there. Your real worth is in direct proportion to what you understand about yourself and what you share from yourself.

How about mastering the most important thing there is?

Master yourself and you will surely exceed any physical worth.

*H*appiness
   is not a thing outside you.
   It is not a car, a house,
   or a fancy piece of jewelry.
   It is, however, found inside of you.
   By your works
   you will find your happiness.
   It is better to give than receive.
   Because you do receive
   each time you give,
   not of outside material things,
   but of yourself, your greatest treasure.

How many times have you worked for a material possession only to find it was more fun working for it than possessing it?

It is certainly not wrong to have possessions. However, it is when the possessions possess you.

Often the things you give from within mean the most in life. The little things you do can have a long-lasting effect on people, like saying good morning, giving a smile or complimenting someone. These little things may be freely given but worth their weight in gold.

Many times we do not have the opportunity to see in others the happiness that results from sharing a beautiful thought.

Do not underestimate the power of your thoughts and how they affect others.

When you have realized the price of a beautiful thought given from one person to another, you will have received a rare gift everyone can enjoy.

*Seek not
to measure yourself,
except
by that which you have inside.*

Measure yourself by the love, compassion and self-understanding you have within. This is a true measure of your life.

Measuring yourself by the misfortunes of others is not a true measure. The misfortunes of others may show you how fortunate you are, but this does not show you your true wealth. Learn to measure yourself by what you have gained within, not by what others have lost.

Learning to measure your own self-worth takes only time and a willingness to pay attention to what is important in life. What you have in physical possessions is not important. It is who you are without your possessions; that is important!

Find love, compassion and self-understanding; then you will never have to measure your wealth. You will have more than you can ever use.

*A whisper
is not always easy to hear
when your life is full of activity.*

The whisper of your wee small voice is a subtle sound. If you cannot hear the wee small voice within, there is too much activity in your mind.

What is the whisper of your wee small voice saying to you?

You can hear many things in your world within. Listen to the natural beauty of your being, not the noise of the outside world. Let not the noise of the outside world drown out the whisper of who you are.

Is the sound in your mind like the thunder of an approaching storm or like a soft breeze gently touching your mind?

When the outside world is in turmoil, go within. Be quiet and hear the whisper of your mind invite you to a place of peace. This place of peace, that only you can find, is your holy space. All truth is heard from this quiet space. Your true being is what it is and is found in silence. The beginning of your being came from within. Go there for your sanctuary.

Walk quietly through your life, not disturbing others along the way. From a quiet man's path comes a quiet life. While many may see this as a boring existence, they know not what they see, for they cannot hear the whisper of the wise man within.

*H*umble yourself
    before yourself,
    that you may be still and know.

A wise man is always humble because he knows he is a part of everything. He has learned to respect all life. When you understand what it is to be humble, you will see great beauty beyond belief.

There is a place in each one of us that is so beautiful, angels smile in its presence. That presence is who you really are. When you can stand spiritually naked, look at yourself and like what you see, you have achieved a great feat.

Feel good about who you are. It is not wrong to feel good about something done well. It is not wrong to have an ego. Ego is the drive that makes us the best we can be and long for excellence. It is wrong, however, to be proud of something you are not, or something you have not done. This is delusion!

If you think you are better than someone else, your thought alone proves you are not. The only thing you have proven is that you have little understanding of yourself. You may be able to do some things better than another; we all have our own forte. But remember, we have all come from the same source.

Be humble and enjoy the beauty in life. In the process of understanding yourself, you will make your life and the lives of those around you much more beautiful.

*Look
to your soul,
not
down upon it.*

Your soul is who you are in this lifetime. Look to your soul; it is your direction in life.

Your soul knows many things, but for most people the soul seems to speak in a foreign language. Take the time to calm your mind and hear what your language is. The language of who you are is written by you. Write your life in a language you can understand. Study and learn to read and write legibly so you can understand yourself. Your school is within you, in your thoughts.

Be patient with yourself when you experience problems and your thoughts are not clear. Do not get down on yourself when you experience troubling thoughts, because you are disregarding what can help you, the understanding from within your mind and soul.

When you begin to know your thoughts you will begin to know your soul!

*Be at peace
with yourself.
If you are not at peace
with yourself,
you are at peace
with nothing.*

This TRUTH is as clear as it can be!

Everything in your life begins and ends with you. Just as you were born, you will die.

What have you done of spiritual significance between your birth and this moment in time?

If you are not at peace with yourself, you are at peace with nothing.

Learn to maintain a peaceful state of mind at all costs. If you do not, it will cost you in the quality of how you experience life.

The peace on our planet earth must first start with peace within each individual!

How often is peace a place within your mind and your world?

If peace is not a place within you everyday, where do you live?

*"A plant
is a beacon of beauty
in the universe
and is always unfolding,
as is all life."*

Chapter Four
The Beauty of Life

WACHSTETTER

*The beauty of the day
is contingent
upon your seeing it.*

To find anything, you must first be looking for it. If you never take time to see beauty, it will not exist in your life.

The appreciation of beauty is a very simple thing and yet has such a profound impact in how you experience life.

The beauty you experience in the world is a mirror image of the beauty within yourself. Beauty cannot be seen outside yourself without first being within you.

How much beauty do you experience in your life?

This question will give you many answers if you look closely enough within.

How can you fully experience the beauty of the outside world if you know not of the beauty of your inside world?

Within and beyond normal outward senses is a playground few choose to look upon. Why? Because few follow the pathway within—a pathway of beauty beyond words. Relax your outward senses and you will find the more subtle senses of beauty within, a place only you can find.

Find beauty within and you will find beauty everywhere.

*What you find in your mind
is what you put there.
Put good things in there.*

Greet each sunrise with a thought of beauty about what the day will bring. Waking up with the thought, "What do I have to do today?" will place a weight on you before you even get out of bed.

There is always something to be enjoyed in any experience when you look for it. You cannot control the world outside you, but you can choose what you will bring into yourself and what you will remember about the day.

If you do not see anything of value in your life, begin today and everyday thereafter by finding one thing of beauty until it becomes a habit.

Each time you experience beauty, you will notice a warm feeling that is hard to put into words. These feelings will show you the wonder of life. You will see for yourself that the accumulation of these feelings will give you a love for life. It is the experience of these feelings that makes life important. When you experience a love for life, you will enjoy your life and know it has great meaning.

If you never look for beauty, who is the person that really misses out?

A flower
is only a thing of beauty
when you see it as such.

If you do not take the time to look for flowers, you will never see them.

An interesting thing happens while you are in the appreciation of beauty; all your problems and worries seem to disappear in the moment. Find more of these moments.

Take time to smell the flowers. This is an ancient truth.

There are flowers everywhere. Does this make them any less beautiful?

Make it a point to look at one flower each day, and you will have something beautiful to remember about every day of your life.

If you do not see the beauty in you and around you, you are missing out on the very essence of spiritual and physical life.

From a natural state of beauty, you will not only see the beauty in all flowers, but in all things.

*If you can see
the beauty of the world,
you will understand
it is there for you.*

An interesting thing happens as you begin to deliberately see more beauty in your life; you see a deeper meaning in it. You begin to see that the beauty of the world is a fragile thing, and from the appreciation of that beauty, you see that all of nature is there to enjoy.

Those individuals who appreciate beauty love to surround themselves with it. Those who do not understand beauty often destroy it or cannot bear to have it around. The dividing line between those who love and those who destroy is in the appreciation of life.

When mankind recognizes that the appreciation of life and beauty is more important than material gain, we will have taken a giant step.

Find beauty in life and you will have taken a step. From seeing you take a step, perhaps it will inspire another to take a step.

If you can understand the beauty within you, you will understand that the beauty of the world is there for you.

*Hold nature
in your hand.
It shows you
how you hold yourself.*

All wise men throughout time share this characteristic—a love for nature! If you have love for yourself, you will love nature; you will understand you are part of it. Flowing with nature is a way to understand her secrets. Destroying something before we have a chance to understand it is the mark of a fool.

When we, because of stupidity or lack of awareness, lose a species of plant or animal life, we have lost the appreciation of something irreplaceable. Nature is something no man can ever create. Destroy not what you cannot create.

We live in a finite space on this planet we call earth. The earth is alive, alive with us. If we pollute or destroy our environment, where can we go?

In the understanding of nature there is an understanding of yourself.

Hold nature in your hand and you will see how you hold yourself.

We must take care of ourselves first or we will not take care of the only home we have.

While the tree is bare in the winter,
the beauty is still sufficient unto itself.
As the seasons change,
so does the beauty subtly change,
moment by moment,
day by day, year by year.
The beauty is sufficient unto itself,
as is your beauty.
All of nature
has something to teach us,
mostly, we are part of it.

We can learn so much from nature if we observe how everything changes with time.

It is in appreciating the subtle change in life that holds nature's secrets. It is most wise to move slowly and observe the subtle changes in you.

Every day, just as a tree grows, so do we as beings. As you change, observe how your beauty changes.

Within change is the beauty of life's mysteries. The mysterious thing called life is not a mystery at all but a natural evolution toward perfection.

Truly, it can be said that within an individual's mind is an individual's true nature.

How much of your own true nature do you understand?

I once had a butterfly come to my finger.
I was overjoyed he had come to visit me.
I wondered in my mind
as I looked and held the butterfly.
Many thoughts ran through my mind
as I marveled at the great beauty
of the magnificent butterfly.
I thought about beauty and what it is,
but as I tried to put it into words,
it seemed to elude me.
For the words had no meaning
compared to the experience.
Such is life.

The next time you see a butterfly, take a few moments to enjoy its simple beauty and you will find yourself not only enjoying the moment, but filling your mind with thoughts that will last a lifetime.

If everyone would learn to appreciate beauty on this level, the world would be a wonderful place. You cannot give the appreciation of life and beauty to anyone, but you can inspire others with your own beauty to see it for themselves.

Many people talk about the wonderful things they plan to do, but did the plans turn into reality?

Do not merely talk about doing beautiful things. Do them, experience them, so life will not elude you.

*The writing of your life
is in its days.
The days in which you live
are your life.
The life in which you live
is you.
Altogether, you are your life.*

Your life is like a novel and you are the author, free to write any way you choose. Make your novel about you and you can be sure it will be interesting to read.

The writing of your life is in how you live your life. Have you taken the time to write beauty into your life?

The days of your life are a complete record of who you are up until this moment in time. Remember, when you are the one writing the script, the outcome is up to you.

Do you like what you have written?

Written within you is a catalog of anything you desire. The mental notes can be that of garbage or that which is noteworthy.

Are you making a garbage pile or are you collecting notes for the novel of a lifetime?

The smile on your face that you receive from time to time, how is it that it should be written?

Between the smile written on your face and the garbage is written your life.

How much of each do you have?

A beautiful way of living
is a state of mind,
not a place.

You may be in the most beautiful place on earth, but if you are not in a beautiful state of mind, you may not see it at all.

Think back to a time when you could not see the beauty in life and how the world looked through your eyes.

Where did this frame of mind come from?

Where did your negative thoughts come from?

Negative thoughts come from an inability to deal with something in your life, in other words, a lack of mental control and understanding on your part. Your part is to understand why you do not understand.

Lack of mental control is the proverbial darkness that haunts most people. Working on your imperfections is not an easy thing to do, but it is what you are here to do. By stilling your mind you will begin to see your imperfections for what they are—disharmony. By recognizing the imperfections in yourself you can learn to pull them like weeds in a garden.

Make your mind a place you can work in freely. Have patience and learn to free yourself from the weeds of disharmony through introspection and contemplation. In time, you will realize that a beautiful way of living is a state of mind, not a place.

When you see yourself
totally beautiful,
you have arrived at your destination.

In seeing yourself totally beautiful you will see heaven, here and now.

Jesus said, "The kingdom of God is within you."

Heaven, or the kingdom of God, is everywhere you experience love and the beauty of life.

Heaven is experienced within you and enjoyed outside you. Heaven is a state of mind, not a place. Heaven is everywhere you see beauty. Heaven is in the beautiful moments we experience in our minds, by our thoughts and expressed through our lives.

The choice to see your destination is up to you. If you choose to be blind of mind, your heavenly destination will be hard to find.

Live a life of love, beauty and self-understanding, then you will not have to look for heaven; heaven will have found you.

"*There* are many words
to be said
about this or that,
but when love
is not one of them,
oh what an emptiness
it can bring you."

WACHTSTETTER

*Give to yourself
the gift of love
and no other gift is needed.*

Love is the most important thing you can cultivate in your life.

If you do not have love within you, what are you giving to those around you?

If you do not plant thoughts of love each day, what will grow in your life?

Love does not mysteriously come from outside you. It is nurtured within by thoughts of kindness, caring and self-understanding.

The giving and receiving of love is the greatest of all lessons we are here to learn. When you can love freely and not expect anything in return, you will have accomplished something quite profound.

The seeds of love come in many ways, and they are everywhere, but you must first find them within. Give to yourself love and you will become it.

We must find love in our hearts and minds. Only then will it materialize in our lives. Tend and grow love inside yourself and you will always have the gift of love to give.

*When you reach your hand
to another,
do so with love.
It will rarely be refused.*

How can you refuse what is an essential part of you?

Love is a part of everyone who lives and breathes. Love is a force that binds all people together like drops of water in a mighty ocean.

How can you not be of love?

If you do not see love within, you have not looked.

From time to time the love you give may not always be wanted, but there is a lesson in this. Give what a person is willing to accept, not just what you want to give. You may very well overwhelm the person and drive them away. Learn to give with sensitivity. It will be easier for you and others to handle. If all a person wants is a thimble full of love, so be it.

If you cross paths with someone who does not want to receive love, what do you do?

Allow them space! Is this not love also?

G*ive*
to yourself
that
which is yours to give.

Within you is the ability to give yourself all the love you could ever imagine.

We are all contained within our own mental boundaries, each according to our own individual awareness. Many people live bound by the world outside them because they know not of an inside world. In order to bring a sense of stability into their lives, people cling to the outside world to control how they feel. They try to give to themselves a sense of love and well-being, and yet it is largely beyond their control because their love is based outside them.

Try this exercise: Close your eyes for a minute and feel where your thinking is centered. You will notice that your thoughts originate from behind your eyes to the middle of your head. This is a plane of awareness between your inside world and your outside world and is your center. From this point allow yourself to reflect inward; this is your inside world and where love is experienced. Return to the center of your thinking and reflect outward away from yourself; this is the outside world.

Take time each day to reflect inward. From inward reflection, you begin to live from within yourself, where love and contentment are found.

Give to yourself that which is yours to give, what everyone is looking for in their life—love and contentment.

Let life
seep into you,
and love
flow out of you.

The beauty of the outside world has much to share with us, let its subtleness seep into you.

Each day our minds take in and process many thoughts and ideas, but after an experience has entered our minds, what ends up flowing out?

How frequently does the expression of love flow out of you?

We have all had feelings of love that are very hard to explain or put into words. These feelings can lift your spirits and help brighten your day. You may notice these feelings at any time—when sharing with a friend, while listening to a song, admiring a beautiful landscape or simply while daydreaming. Fill your mind with as many beautiful and loving thoughts as you can.

There are many ways to experience love, but if your life is like a rushing river, it will be clouded with too much movement. Slow the river of life to a gentle brook.

Love is a universal language beyond words, an experience complete unto itself. Allow the experience of love into your life and the same will flow out.

When you reach your hand
out to another,
do so
with an open and giving hand,
or do not reach out at all.

Think about how you give what you give, not only to others, but to yourself.

Give to others because you want to share, not because you feel you have to.

Is giving out of obligation really giving?

When you give with strings attached, you are not giving. You are trading something you have for something you want. You have made what you gave some form of business. If it is business you are doing, that's fine, but you are not giving. Make it a point to see clearly what business is and what business is not.

Take it upon yourself to give from your heart with no strings attached to get in the way of love and friendship.

When you feel and know what it is like to truly give from the heart, you will know that what you have given is more profitable than any business deal.

*W*alk with your heart
in your mind,
and you will never
say something
you don't mean.

You will rarely say something you are sorry for when your heart and your mind work as one, because your heart will tell your mind it is wrong before you say it.

If you think from your mind what you feel in your heart, you will see and feel in a more compassionate and loving way.

We have all said things we did not mean and then regretted it. Think about what it is you are thinking about, before you speak, so you will not regret what you say. If you lose control, try to understand why you have lost control, instead of lashing out at someone.

There is a well-known saying, "We always hurt the ones we love because they will understand." Try to never let this happen to loved ones, or for that matter, to anyone! Take some time to be by yourself when you are upset with something in your life. Go for a walk, calm your mind, and have a talk with yourself until you regain control. When you are yourself again, look carefully at your feelings and actions and ask yourself, "Why is it I have so much anger?" Trace the roots of anger back to its past and you will find your answer. When your heart is tempering your mind, the fire of anger will become dimly lit and can then be put out.

Just as you are one person, let also your heart and mind be as one.

The wise man respects all life.
He who is kind, and has a kind heart,
will in turn be greeted with kindness.
For being in a world
in which your heart is full of love,
you will be where people dream to be.
Be free, by being in control of your life
and at peace with yourself.
Seek self-understanding
and the world sits at your feet.

The pathway upon which you walk is many times riddled with stones that can trip you up and throw you off balance. These stones represent the problems in your life. The stones that plague most people are not from outside themselves, but from the negative emotions of their own thoughts.

While many see the pathway outside themselves as the only pathway, alas it is not true, for the pathway of knowing is from within you. Look to this pathway for the light that will guide you. Seek and find the light of awareness and all shadows of darkness will disappear.

Seek self-understanding and you will find inner-peace and love. From understanding yourself, you will see many markers along the pathway that denote a true spiritual person. Love, self-understanding and compassion for all living creatures are a few signs to look for. One day we will all come to the understanding that we are of love. Live a life reaching toward the goal of being absolute love.

When you walk with love, compassion and self-understanding long enough, you will know why the wise man respects all life.

The bridges that one crosses
in his lifetime are many
and the way not always easy.
Would you not fear an action
that you did not do,
or wonder about it
in a dark corner of your mind?
Seek to find the darkness in your mind.
But, be very sure you are not creating it.
Believing in yourself is the first step
to eradicating the darkness.
If you do not put in the time
to understand yourself,
you have put in nothing.

Seeking darkness is confronting fear, face to face. Fear will block your ability to see anything clearly.

Do not be afraid of the darkness within that you may find from time to time. Look to the light of awareness inside and see that darkness is just fear of the unknown. Use the light from your own awareness to cast out the shadows of fear in your mind. When your mind has the light of understanding, there are no hidden corners for the darkness of fear to hide.

The darkness of unknowing is a sad thing. It imprisons people in their own thoughts. When you are imprisoned by your own thoughts, you know not what direction to go or what direction you have come from. The sadness is when you do not even know you are in the darkness.

Find the wee small light within. You will recognize it at first as a feeling, a feeling of love. This feeling will lead to knowing. When you know the feeling of love, you will not need to seek it; you will be it. Between fear and love is the distance of life.

How far have you travelled toward love?

It is important
to know where one stands in life.
If one does not know where one stands,
one can often feel lost.
Do not use material objects
as points of reference,
for they can be lost or stolen.
Use your spiritual values.
They can never be taken away.

This is a teaching about a small boy whose father was very selfish and spent most of his time acquiring possessions. The father spent little time with his young son. A short time later the boy's father was killed in an accident. The boy cried because he did not understand his father's death. He thought something was wrong with him and wondered why his father had spent so much time playing with his things and not with him. The boy asked his mother, "Why did he spend so much time playing with his things and not with me? They were not even alive!"

From the mouths of babes come words of wisdom. In losing the ability to see what is really important in life, one has lost something that can never be replaced, the loving time spent with another individual. How can you measure this loss?

What is the measure of something that can never be regained?

*T*he wonders of life
are what life is about,
not what people have,
but what people do.

Possessions can hardly be as valuable as life itself.

Possessions are inanimate and cannot express feelings or thoughts.

The appreciation of fine things is beautiful, but let things be things.

Love people and use things.

Do not use people and love things.

Things can bring you comfort, but they will not bring you peace of mind.

Things cannot give love and things cannot return love.

If love is what you are looking for, do not possess it. For in the possession you have just lost it. Love cannot be held in the hand. It is felt from the heart.

Weigh your love and possessions and see how much each weighs. Leave the weight of the outside world in it; then you need not carry it. Carry love which only exists in your heart, because its weight is not of this physical world.

If things become more important than love, take a serious look at your life.

*W*hat good
is the most beautiful chalice
in the world,
when you are thirsty
and the chalice is empty?

All the money in the world cannot buy one ounce of love or spirituality, but if you open your heart and mind to love, it is free.

Without money or possessions who are you?

Are you rich or are you poor?

Free yourself from the distractions of money and possessions and discover what is really important, the giving and receiving of love. You may have heard this many times before, but what does it really mean?

Within you is one of the most beautiful oases you will ever find; it is absolute love. Seek the oasis within your heart, mind and soul. If you cannot find your oasis, you are living in a desert. Walk out of the desert, into the openness of your mind, and you will see your oasis. Start your journey by loving yourself each day. Fill your chalice with love from your oasis within so when you meet others who are thirsty on the road of life, you have something to share.

When everyone has found their own oasis, no one will ever go thirsty again.

*The blessing you seek
is your own blessing,
from yourself
to yourself.*

A blessing given to yourself each morning is a blessing received.

The blessing in life is in what you do with your life.

Do you love what you do in your life?

Remember always, the blessing of life is upon those who love.

Love is within you and all around you, but you must first recognize it, then you become it.

The authority to give a blessing comes not from a clergyman but from love within.

Can you think of anyone who is more blessed than someone who is full of love?

If you can give love without condition, is not a blessing already upon you?

Real and complete love is sufficient unto itself.

Give yourself a blessing each day by giving to yourself the most important thing you can, the gift of love.

"*Flow with the winds
of time, yielding
to the currents of life.
Let your worries fall away
like the leaves of an
autumn tree following
the way of nature.
Let the winds of time
carry you
along your way.*"

WACHSTETTER

As the winds of time
blow across your mind,
let them be soft and gentle,
caressing your soul.
Let the winds carry you
on your pathway,
not disturb it.

Change on your pathway is like following the seasons. You can no more force the seasons than you can force change; you are in it already. Be content with change; know you are moving in the direction you want to go.

If you are living your life in harmony, you will have time to do everything; life will get easier, not harder. Unless of course, you are foolish and do not learn from your mistakes. Mistakes are a part of everyone's life and how we learn. But remember, a mistake is not a mistake when you have learned from it. The mistake has become the lesson. Let the winds of time whisper the secrets of living to you, so mistakes become fewer and fewer.

It is a beautiful feeling as the lessons of life gently nudge you along your way to a more complete understanding of yourself.

Control the winds of time in how you use time, not in trying to control time itself. Let the winds of time caress your soul, not disturb it.

A day is sufficient unto itself.
The question is:
What did you do with it?

Each day is a golden gem and will never come again. Make each day something of great beauty to remember. With each sunrise is an opportunity to do something you may have never done before. The only things in life you will ever regret are the things you did not do.

Do not put off until tomorrow what you can do today.

Do in life what makes you feel good inside. Within your mind is your day and your world; it is seen out there but understood in here. From the understanding of yourself will come the understanding of your world.

Relax, go slow!

Enjoy yourself.

Move at a pace that is comfortable to you.

The day is sufficient unto itself but are you sufficiently pleased with what you have done with your day?

*To live
for another day
is the mark of a fool.
You are only fooling yourself.*

The sands of time neither wait for a fool nor a saint. The fool deludes himself in thinking happenstance or good luck will come his way, while the saint knows each step and is content with that step. Within the knowing of each human is this range of using time. Where do you fit in?

Another day may as well be a world away. Between the time you spend in your inside world and the time you spend in your outside world is your real world.

If you are living for tomorrow, you are not living today. The promise of tomorrow is not worth half as much as today. Take care of today and tomorrow will take care of itself.

This moment will never come again. You are only fooling yourself if you think it will.

The sands of time
are at your beck and call
when you understand the hidden meaning
in their individual grains.
It is in trying to grab too much
that you lose
the individual feeling in each grain.
Learn to count each individual grain;
then, and only then,
will you understand time's true meaning.
Within each second of each minute
is time's true meaning
and the meaning of who you are.

When the sands of time are slipping too quickly through your fingers, it is because you are trying to hold too much. Your hands were meant to hold a handful because that's what hands hold. Is not all you can hold enough?

When you can slow your mind enough to feel each second, you begin to see and appreciate a different you and a different world. From your mind comes your sense of time. From your senses come the subtleties and nuances of what time is.

What does time feel like to you?

Do you and time have the same feeling?

Are you in sync with time?

What do you do with your time that helps you understand yourself?

Learn to count each individual grain of time; then, and only then, will you understand time's true meaning and your connection to it.

Walking
with your bare feet in the sand
will measure time better
than the hands of a clock.

In a time when people live by the hands of a clock instead of by their own hands, it is hard to truly sense what time is really about.

With technology has come machines which give us more time to do what we want. But instead of giving more time to ourselves, many people have just added more things to do in their day.

Time was invented by man and has done more to shackle him than set him free.

If you do not use the clock to give you time, you may very well become a slave to it.

Your work in the outside world is an important part of your life, but it is not what you came here to do. You are not here to be a slave to a clock or to your work. You are here to learn about yourself and enjoy yourself along the way.

Should not all of us make our lives a walk on the beach, instead of just moving from point A to point B?

Experience time! Do not just move through it. The time you enjoy is a true measure of quality time.

Take time for yourself or time may become something else, something you may not want to experience.

*T*ime to yourself
is yours.
Otherwise,
it is something else.

The something else in life for most people is work. Be happy in your work or change your work. You will be happier with yourself and everyone around you.

If you do not like what you are doing and feel you cannot change your work, you are not really trying; there are always ways.

Take steps each day toward finding what it is you want to do in life. Search your mind for what you like to do and pursue it.

We all have a niche in this world, but a niche does not hunt for you; you must hunt for it. Try hunting inside yourself.

Have you not noticed that your niche is you?

If you cannot find you, how will you find your niche?

Take time to find you and you will find your niche.

$\mathcal{P}$*atience!*
The trees do not change
their leaves in one day.

There are those who do not want to change and there are those who want to change too quickly. In the center is moderation and the middle pathway. Follow this pathway! Impatience will only bring you frustration and confusion.

Flow with changes in your life and you will be where you should be—content with your life.

Make small changes each day, not major ones.

Major changes can also be major mistakes.

Small changes are much easier to correct and much more comfortable to live with, if you are wrong.

Find what feels natural and comfortable within and accomplishments will replace mistakes.

The seasons of nature change naturally. So should we!

Be comfortable with yourself. If being comfortable with yourself does not come naturally, change! It is unnatural to be uncomfortable with yourself.

*D*o not be so impatient with yourself
that you cannot see the light
of your own pathway,
by a shadow of your own doubt!

Be careful not to get in your own way, by being impatient. Impatience creates a fog so dense it is hard to see the pathway upon which you walk.

Doubt is something that surrounds all people from time to time and is a part of everyone's pathway.

We will all have doubt, but the question is: What will you do about it?

When you find yourself in doubt, stand still and center yourself. The clouds of doubt will disappear when you see the clarity of your own thoughts. Doubt is only healthy when it helps you to find the answer you seek. Doubt will always tell you one thing—you do not understand something. This realization is good. It is telling you to slow down so you do not make a mistake. When doubt no longer clouds your awareness, clarity will reveal your answer.

*Because you cannot do it today,
does not mean
you cannot do it tomorrow.*

Although it is today that counts, DO NOT GIVE UP. Anything worth doing well takes time.

There is much to learn and do in life; this is where patience comes in. Patience is not just a word but a wise use of time.

If you look where you are, you will see you are exactly where you have put yourself. You are not a puppet on a stage with someone pulling your strings. The only stage you are on is the stage you have made for yourself. If you do not like where you have put yourself, take steps to change it.

When you do not know where to stand, stand some place that is comfortable. With a free mind contemplate your situation. The answers will come when you are patient enough to see them.

Be patient.
Time moves at its own speed
and there is nothing you can do about it,
but use it wisely.

A wise old saying is: "In time and on time."

Use time wisely by getting in touch with how fast you move from one experience to another. Knowing when to move and when to be patient is a valuable skill. Do not hurry. The moment you left behind is the same moment ahead. The moments are all the same. What is different is you.

There are many things you can do, but if you are in a hurry, you miss out on the moment and the very thing you are doing.

Be mindful of each moment in your day. SLOW DOWN!

Your journey is not only about arriving at your destination. The journey is the journey. The end is not the journey.

The destination will be what it will be, but did you enjoy the way?

Age
can tell you many things,
if you listen.
If not, you grow old.

As a tree grows older, so does its beauty. Is it not a marvel to see something that has stood the test of time and is of great beauty?

It is the cultivation of beauty and awareness which brings us to the place we long to be, happy and content with our lives.

If you do not learn from life's lessons, you will grow old before your time. Old age is not necessarily synonymous with wisdom. Wisdom comes from the love of life, not in the measure of one's years.

As you grow older in years, do not fight change but recognize change for what it is. If you are not growing, you are in a habitual pattern. If you are in a pattern you do not want to leave because you fear change, your life will become hard and brittle.

Take it upon yourself to listen to your years, so that as you age, you become wise, not old and foolish. When you listen carefully to your life you will feel something—the movement of change.

Is your movement beautiful?

Age will tell you many things, if you are listening. Most importantly, that life has great meaning and beauty.

*W*hen you are old enough
to see the wisdom of your age,
you will see how beautiful it really is.

The wisdom of your age is in the appreciation of your life. Do things that will better your life and you will experience more life and less existence. Boredom with life is a sign you are living in a black and white existence.

Have you ever noticed that negative thoughts seem to appear in black and white, while beautiful, fulfilling thoughts seem to be in color?

Find harmony within and you will see a depth in life, not just the same old day after day. The aspects of your personality that make you a more harmonious person are gems of wisdom. When you see the wisdom of who you are and appreciate it, you will have found within you priceless riches.

If harmony within determined what age you were, how old would you be?

The leaves of the trees are green,
then they turn brown, fall off and die.
Such is the cycle of nature.
Your nature is eternal, eternal in nature.
In the grand scheme of things,
you are only here in the blink of an eye,
and yet, the moment can be eternal.
Which do you choose in your life. . .
the eternal moment or the blink of an eye?

This moment is all there is! The choice of what to do with it is up to you. When you are living in the moment, it is eternal. When you are not living in the moment, you are in the past or in a dream.

Are you reliving the past trying to recapture yesterday, or living in a dream world hoping tomorrow will get better?

It is easy to get comfortable reliving past events or living in a future dream world by not wanting to face the moment. You will have to face everything in your life one day. Really look at yourself. Make this moment better and every moment will be better. Really think about this!

By facing your life you find your true nature within. Between the energy it takes to face yourself and the full experience of life is the true meaning you seek.

Live each day and your life will not be gone in the blink of an eye but a continuation of nature's eternal moment.

As the clock ticks away,
what do the seconds of the day mean?
Do they mean anything?
Within time is your experience of life.
The further along the pathway you are,
the more the moments mean.
If you do not value the moment,
this will tell you; you have much to learn.
The clock of your life is you.
Do you know what time it is?

Time starts taking on new meaning as you become a student of yourself. Your time becomes the most important thing in your life.

Time is the one thing we are all involved in. The question is: How much are you involved in it?

Time is something you spend everyday, but it cannot be bought at any price. You spend time on everything: yourself, loved ones, family, friends. The time in your life is priceless. What determines what you spend your time on?

You are the only one who can decide time's true value. We all have a limited amount of time. Learn its value today, do not wait until the last day of your life.

If tomorrow were your last day and you could buy another, how much would it be worth?

"*Your lessons*
are in your hands,
not mine.
I can no more tell you
what to say
than I can tell you
what to do;
it is your life,
your lessons to learn."

Learn to look within
and around yourself,
so that you might learn
something new each day.

If you are not learning something new each day, you are not growing. Anything that does not grow stagnates or dies. Personal growth is anything learned about yourself and the world around you.

Opening your mind is like opening a book you have not fully read. This book is a technical manual. It is a book of commands. How many commands do you control?

Is your book a pamphlet or an encyclopedia? This book is you. How much do you know about it?

Your mind is like one of many muscles in the body; it needs to be exercised to work properly. The difference between your mind and other muscles is that your mind controls all others. How strong or weak is your mind?

Learning is one of many mental exercises. Has the idea of doing mental exercises each day ever entered your mind?

Let not the idea only enter but also work-out. The first part of any work-out is to do it!

Often,
it is more important to understand
why you want to learn,
than the knowledge itself.

There is much wisdom in wanting to learn. If you do not want to learn, this is your first mistake. Your mistakes will keep repeating until you learn from them. Think about this!

Your want to learn and understand your life is your pathway.

If you are not learning on your pathway, what direction are you going?

If you choose not to learn, the by-product will be ignorance. There is a saying, "Ignorance is bliss." Ignorance is ignorance and is born from laziness, not bliss. Just because you are unaware of something does not mean it does not exist.

Born from love is the realization of who you are and your pathway to bliss. When you have the soft feeling of love within, you will not have to wonder where bliss is. Bliss will be you.

*From the understanding
of not understanding
comes understanding.*

One must first admit that he does not understand, to begin to understand. From the understanding of yourself will come all spiritual understanding.

There are many schools of thought in the world, but there is no school as complete as the thoughts you can think. No one can think for you. Your answers in life are in the thoughts you think. The greatest learning institution in the world is within your own mind.

What do your thoughts teach you?

Understanding is difficult in an uncontrolled mind. By quieting your mind you will find your blackboard. A chalkboard full of writing is difficult to learn from because nothing is clear! Wipe the chalkboard clean by stilling your mind so you can see what you are thinking. Then it will be easier to study.

From understanding your mind will come all understanding. Learn to still your mind and see!

*If someone set a mental boundary
and you could see beyond it,
would you not cross?*

Your own mental boundary is a limitation you have placed on your own mind. It is in testing the limits of our boundaries that we learn.

All great minds who could see beyond what others saw were considered strange when they introduced a new idea. If their own fear or the fear of what other's might think stopped them, where would we be today?

Do not be afraid to try something different simply because someone has said it cannot be done. We will all make mistakes. Making mistakes is mankind's trademark; it is how we learn. When you can acknowledge you have made a mistake, you have taken a giant step in learning.

Let's all work to recognize our problems and make mankind's trademark one of understanding rather than making mistakes. It is better to have tried and failed, than to have not tried and always wondered what might have been.

What accomplishments ever came from a mind that was not allowed to grow?

The limits of your growth are only determined by you and your ability to think clearly.

It is in the attempt
that brings about the trying.
It is in the trying
that brings about the doing.
And it is the doing
that brings about the being.

Everything you do in life will happen step-by-step. Just as a student moves from one grade to the next, so your learning process in life continues from one day to the next.

When we try something new it is usually an attempt. As you sincerely attempt something, you begin to really try. Once you seriously try, you begin doing it. After doing something time after time, you begin to get very good, until one day what you are doing becomes second nature and you are being what you are doing. The doing becomes the being. Such is the way of learning.

This step-by-step teaching will work in all aspects of your life. It will only fail if you do not attempt to try.

Take steps each day to find out a little bit more about yourself. Then one day you will become aware that who you are is the same as who you are being.

In whatever you do, you must be committed.

Are you committed to making your life better?

How do you handle your commitments?

A commitment will cease to be a commitment

when you enjoy doing it,

because you would not think to do otherwise.

A commitment is set by <u>your</u> timetable,

not forever.

Forever is an awfully long time.

How did you learn to do anything? By committing to do it, for the right amount of time, not all time.

One of the hardest things people struggle with are commitments. Really think about what you are doing when you decide to commit to someone or something. Ask yourself, "Does this feel right or wrong?" If it feels wrong, take time with the decision, until you know what feels right and what to do next.

A commitment is not something set in stone; stones do not grow. If there is no growth in something you commit to, it is time to reevaluate the commitment.

If your commitment does not produce beautiful fruit, what good is it?

If it is not good why continue your commitment?

Learn from commitments; do not become a slave to them.

Pay close attention to this statement, "A commitment will cease to be a commitment when you enjoy doing it, because you would not think to do otherwise."

You
are an example of life.
You must decide of what!

What are you an example of in your life?

If you have done what is right, your life will be in harmony. You will be an example of what is right, not what is wrong.

Many people live their lives looking back over their shoulder to things they have done in the past. Do what is right and the only reason for looking back will be to see beautiful memories.

Everyone knows what is right and what is wrong.

Why choose wrongly?

You know when you choose wrongly. It feels wrong!

Practice paying attention to your feelings and you will begin to see more clearly what they are trying to tell you.

It is you who must question your feelings to discover why you do what you do. The question is a pathway to the answer. It is from clear answers that we build a foundation of trust in our lives.

If you cannot trust yourself, what are you an example of?

You could be doing other things,
but do those things
that you want to do.

There are things you have to do to be responsible, but there are many other times when you have a choice. One of the things that separates people from animals is our ability to make choices. You have a powerful ability as a human being. Use it wisely and you will be where you want to be, not just going through life without control or purpose.

The decisions within an individual are many times complicated by the "have-tos" and the "I cannots". Do not limit yourself by this thinking.

The milestones that are important are not the physical ones but the little, subtle feelings along the way. Far too often people look to the wrong guideline, a guideline which is directed from outside them.

Do what you want to do in life, not what someone else wants you to do.

There are so many things you can do. Why do you hold back?

*P*eople need not know
what you are experiencing.
*Y*ou need to know
what you are experiencing.

It is no one's business what you do in your life, as long as you do not interfere with anyone else's life. Far too many people involve themselves in what others are doing. Your experience of life is yours—not anyone else's. Be about your own life. When you have made your life into something of beauty, then you can share that beauty with all who wish to enjoy it.

NON-INTERFERENCE is a natural law in play in the physical and spiritual universe at all times, whether or not you are aware of it. Interference is deliberately placing something in another's pathway to trip them up or to make them do something that they would not normally do.

A common result of breaking the law of non-interference is retaliation. Another common result is pain. When you try to control another's life, be it friends or loved ones, you can cause yourself and them great pain because you have interfered in their life.

True spiritual laws are laws for a simple reason—break them and disharmony will not be far away.

Non-interference is a major law in the universe. When people finally accept this spiritual law as truth, the lamb will finally be able to lie down with the lion in peace.

*Do not expect or think things
should be a certain way.
They never or rarely are.
It is wonderful to plan,
but be able to move freely.
If your plans change
because of what you cannot control,
what do you do?*

A wise man does not try to control something outside himself. He flows with life, which is a way to harmony within him and his surroundings. He sees with a clear mind what is for his highest and best good.

A wise teacher can easily see why a student has a difficult time because he came by way of the student. The teacher and the student are one.

One day I was pondering a difficult situation which was affecting my whole life, when my teacher said, "The situation is not important my son; what is important is how you deal with it."

Think back to when you had a problem. Did you think you were the first person to experience that problem?

There is always a solution to a problem. Some problems just take more time to solve. Learn to move freely with your thinking. Many times the solution to our problem is so close yet we do not see it. Stand back and give your mind some space and time to solve the problem. You simply may be trying too hard!

One day
while talking with a wise teacher,
he asked,
"How are you?"
I replied,
"I am a little down and depressed."
The teacher then asked,
"Is this because of your control,
or no control?"

There will be times in your life when you may be a little down and a little depressed.

When you are in this state of mind, how is it you change to the place you wish to be?

Does the depression come from within you or outside you?

Within the depression is the answer and the way to change. Watch carefully the source of the depression and your attachment to it. When you can understand why you are holding onto something, then you will see how you can free yourself from it. From learning detachment comes the ability to free yourself from depression.

Who really controls the feelings in your life?

If you are not in control, what direction are you going?

If your control is no control, who then chooses?

If you do not choose, circumstance will be your choice.

Blessed
   is he who finds himself
   and wishes to share
   what is found with the world.

Far too often people do not get what they want in life because of their own burdens. The futility of self-inflicted pain is neither noble nor wise but a lack of awareness.

Learn to be your own best friend and there will never be a need to be your own worst enemy. A wise teacher said to me, "If you are your own worst enemy, you have no defense." Defend yourself against harmful outside things and confront the painful inside things; these burdens you cannot run away from. If each person would carry their own responsibility, a great burden would be lifted from the planet.

The way and the truth is within. It has always been so and will always be so. When you have learned to live in the truth, you will never need to defend yourself again.

When you have taken care of yourself, you will have time to take care of others. The want to care for others is a beautiful thing called compassion. When compassion is coupled with spiritual understanding, great strides will be made in our world.

*Shaky is a life
that holds onto possessions
and not onto life.
It is like trying to hold onto you
when you are not you.*

The only possession you can ever really hold onto is you.

Shallow is a life spent attaining the wrong riches. Your sense of well-being and spiritual depth comes from taking care of the riches within you, not outside you.

When you are only living in the material world, this question often comes to mind: "Is this all there really is?"

We live in a physical world and must, of course, take care of our things, but when outside things become more important than inside things, disharmony will surely be close.

Is it not very sad when someone cannot see the beauty that lies within?

When the beauty within an individual is not found, you are lost. Find your way not in possessions but in what you possess within.

Success is the mark of something done well.
Count your marks and be pleased with them.
As you gain marks,
you gain inner-strength and knowing.
Continue to slow down your mind,
so that you can see more of your life.
It is how much you can comprehend,
not how fast you go.
Success is a mark
on the pathway to enlightenment.

When you have done something that works in your life, success will happen. From each success comes confidence, from confidence and practice come inner-strength and finally, knowing.

As you learn more about your mind, you will understand why slowing your thoughts is important. Your mind can only go so fast and then it becomes scattered. If your mind is scattered, what then is your life?

With practice you will observe from slowed thoughts how your life will naturally settle to a level that is comfortable for you. This comfortable feeling within is your center.

If you are going nowhere fast, slow down. The quality of life is in the moment not in how much you can do in a day. If you do not learn patience, you will simply be uncomfortable.

The speed at which you move on your pathway is not important; what is important is how much you can comprehend about it.

The pats on the back you receive are nothing compared to what you have done for yourself.

The pats on the back you receive from time to time are great but not nearly as important as what you have accomplished yourself.

Is not your personal accomplishment more important than someone praising you for it?

If you are seeking approval outside yourself for something you have done, you are doing things for the wrong reasons. Seeking gratification from outside yourself is disappointment waiting to happen.

For what reason would you need to seek approval in what you do?

Answer this question and you will learn many things about yourself.

Learn to do things in life for no other reason than it is the right thing to do. This is a pathway that leads to contentment.

*Dream not
what is tomorrow.
Dream what is now.*

Why is it some waking dreams come true while others do not?

Each one of us measures our self-worth on varying levels. The beginning of a dream must be based on a feeling that you are worthy to receive it. If you are to make your dreams come about, learn to traverse through the doubts within your mind to the depths of your soul. This is a pathway of turning dreams into reality.

Waking dreams are no more than thoughts that have not been brought into reality. It is the beautiful creation of our thoughts that inspires dreams to come about. Feed your dreams daily with step-by-step thoughts, then take action to make your dreams come true.

Learn to dream what is now, then you will be where you want to be today, not tomorrow. Live your dream a little each day until the dream finally becomes the day. All you will ever have is this moment to bring your dreams about. MAKE YOUR THOUGHTS THINGS!

On the next clear night go outside and wish upon a star, then make that wish come true. Make your wish come true by taking steps each day to bring it about.

It is only from the steps of doing that dreams become reality.

There are many wonders in the world.

Take the time to find them.

Experience life to its fullest.

If you do not,

you are only cheating yourself.

The wonder of any land is not in the land but in the mind seeing it. If you have wonder in your mind, you will see wonder in your life.

Throughout a person's life there are many experiences that can bring about a feeling of wonder. Wonder is a facet within the mind that keeps you young at heart. As people age wonder seems to become a thing of the past, something they experienced when they were children. You do not have to be a child to experience wonder. It is a state of mind, not a state of age. Observe a child. They will teach you many things about wonder that you may have forgotten.

Leave not the wonder of your childhood behind. When the wonder of your childhood has become the wonder in your adult life the world has gained one more wonder.

*Laughter is good
when it comes.
It should come more often.*

On a street corner, in a small town, laughter comes easier because people are easier. When jamming too many people on a street corner, laughter becomes imprisoned within the protective walls of each mind.

The same can be said for you when you jam too many thoughts in your mind; laughter becomes imprisoned. Imprison not laughter. Imprison not your soul. Stop the thought of imprisoning anything within you.

Laughter is never weighed by negative things, negative things are their own weight. We all must do what we must do, but we do not have to be weighed down by it.

Do you not agree people are far too serious?

Feel your laughter with your heart and allow it to flow freely throughout your soul.

*The symbol of happiness
is all around you,
when you are the one
writing the symbol.*

Only you can decide what makes you happy.

All of the decisions you make are made within your mind and expressed through your life. If you want your life to have meaning, think meaningful thoughts that will produce happiness.

Happiness does not seek you out. Seek out the thoughts in life that bring you happiness.

The abstract kind of happiness that most people seek is fleeting. The fleeting comes not from the happiness but from a mind that does not understand where to find true happiness.

Happiness is a state of mind and can be created at any time. Your time of happiness is an individual decision. It is not decided by something or someone outside you. Decide what happiness is by deciding what brings you happiness within.

Be happy with yourself and the symbol of happiness will be beautifully written, not only for you, but also for those who are looking for what you have found.

Happiness is what it is. Are you it?

"*N*ever will you receive
so much
from absolutely nothing
as stillness of mind."

WACHSTETTER

The importance of meditation
is only as important
as you make it in your mind.
How important is your life?
The two are linked,
life and meditation, thought and no thought.
Balance is the result.
Control of your life
is what you are seeking, is it not?
Control your life
through the advent of meditation.

In taking the time to quiet your mind you will learn a profound truth; you cannot clearly observe if you cannot stop the chatter in your mind. In the purest sense— STILL THE MIND.

Learn to still your mind. It is one of the single most important things you can do for yourself, and yet many people are totally unaware of it. Literally make your mind shut up! Meditation is not an easy thing to do and will probably be one of the hardest disciplines you will ever undertake, but if you cannot control your thinking, there will be confusion in your mind. Too many thoughts will conceal the very thing you may be seeking in life. Clear the confusion with stillness and see the light from within your own mind.

Your mind can light your way, but if you cannot find the switch to turn on the light, you will walk around in darkness and not even know it. The switch is meditation, stilling the mind.

Learn to light your pathway with the illumination from your own mind.

With help from yourself, for yourself,

you will see your own way.

It is the only way to truly see your pathway.

Meditation is the sight

that is given to the blind.

A blending of meditation, living and time

is all that is needed

to bring about a happy and fulfilled life.

"How can these help you in your life?"

Meditation—because it is your guiding light

that will help you see the way.

Living—because it is what we are here to do,

Time—because it is essential.

These are keys. What will you do with them?

Meditation is a simple practice but difficult to do.

Sit down, get comfortable and for ten minutes in the morning and evening, go inside yourself and quiet your mind of all thought. You will find that stilling your mind is difficult because your mind has always been in motion.

What direction is that motion taking you?

Meditation will show you the direction you are going. Be persistent and over a period of time you will begin to see subtle results. Life will begin to take on a different meaning. Not that your life will have new meaning, but you will become more aware of what the true meaning is.

MEDITATION PROVIDES A POINT OF REFERENCE. It is a still point from which all can be seen clearly.

Your mind has many keys that open many doors but you must first be able to find the keys before you can use them.

If you do not have twenty minutes in twenty-four hours to take care of your mind, YOU ARE TOO BUSY!

*It is not
the shutting out of thought
that you are trying to achieve,
but an allowing of stillness to happen.*

You cannot force a flower to open and you cannot force your mind to be still. You must allow it to happen.

Remember, and file away this statement: ALLOW STILLNESS TO HAPPEN. This is very important!

Meditation is stillness of the mind in its purest sense. It is from a point right outside of stillness where you find the doorway to realizations. Once you begin to meditate, you begin to have more realizations. This is due to the fact that you are opening up places in your mind you knew not existed. This is the other 90% of your mind. In essence you are opening up your own learning process. Your mind is opening to everything that is life.

From time to time all people have realizations about their life but how is it one realizes who they are?

You will realize who you are through self-study and by allowing your mind to get still over a period of time. Your awareness of who you are will dawn on you like a beautiful sunrise seen over a lifetime, with one exception. The light will be coming from within you, not outside you.

$\mathcal{D}$iligence,

is it in the back of your mind?
Should it not be in your practice?

In the back of our minds, many of us want to be diligent about this or that, but somehow it is difficult to get going and keep going. There is no secret. You just have to do it!

Diligence can apply to many things in your life. In this case it is referring to being diligent about meditating each day.

When you begin to meditate, it will be difficult. Your mind will not want to cooperate. It will seem like there are two minds within you. This is known as the big mind and the small mind. The big mind is you trying to meditate and knows what is for your highest and best good. While the small mind is like an undisciplined child, constantly chattering and needing guidance. Guide the uncontrolled child with discipline.

In the morning and evening simply sit down and take time to still your mind. Be diligent about clearing your mind of unnecessary thoughts and you will understand why meditation is so important.

When you begin to see and enjoy the value in what you are doing, you will meditate every day.

*T*he outside world
is a distraction,
is it not?
Or,
is the distraction within you?

No DISTRACTIONS is one of the natural spiritual laws of the universe. You cannot do anything well if you are distracted. When you become distracted, you are not in full control of what you are doing.

Distractions can come in many forms, from not being able to concentrate on a simple project, to endangering yourself by not paying attention. The law of NO DISTRACTIONS is what it is and is simply part of understanding the physical and spiritual universe in which we live. There is something you can do about distractions; learn CONCENTRATION and MEDITATION—the solution to the problem of distractions.

If you control your mind and how you think, you can control how you deal with the outside world. Then the distractions of the world will be outside you, rather than within you.

Do not let your mind wander,
unless that is what you want it to do.
Practice your practice daily
and it will be daily.
When you look at a flower,
are you looking at a flower
or something that reminds you of something?
Be mindful.
Pay attention to what your mind is doing.
Train your mind to do what you want.
You will be much happier with your mind,
and your mind, much happier with you.

A good exercise to help focus the mind is to concentrate on a flower for a couple of minutes at a time, before or after your meditation, whenever you are most comfortable. While observing the flower look at all parts in fine detail: the color, the texture, the shape, the fragrance, every little nuance of the flower you can find. As you concentrate you may notice thoughts cross your mind other than the flower. Continue to focus on the flower until all you are thinking about is the flower. This is concentration!

When you practice concentration, use persistence as your guide, not frustration.

Concentration is VERY IMPORTANT for the mind to learn.

This exercise will help your mind focus on one thing at a time. You will see how hard it is to not think of anything but the flower but with practice, over time, you will understand why concentration is such a valuable tool.

*It is the persistence
of daily activities
that bring about
a continuity of events
in your life.*

Meditation and concentration are two important disciplines that will help bring about a continuity of events in your life. Meditation and concentration are stillness and thought, the passive and the active. Within this medium is the yin and the yang, the Tao, the middle path and moderation in all things.

From the flowing of one moment into the next will come your pathway. It will probably not come in a blinding flash but in step-by-step realizations. Pay attention to your steps and you will pay attention to what is important. Be patient. Do your practices of concentration and meditation and live your life.

The truth has been said in many lands and at different points in history. The truth has always been the same; it is what it is and can be no more or no less. What is different is the mind perceiving it.

How clear is your perception?

If your perception is not clear, what then of your daily activities?

If your perception is clear your activities will be truthful.

Practice,
practice,
practice,
in moderation!

We all know that practice makes perfect, but practice in moderation.

Moderation is the way to find comfort inside yourself. Use comfort within yourself as a yardstick to measure what moderation is and is not in your life. Many times students will try to do too much too fast and end up getting in their own way. Go slow so you can find a comfortable pace.

Your mind is the most advanced computer there is. Give the mental screen in your mind a rest when it is tired. Take a few minutes to calm your mind. After you have calmed your mind, you will find yourself more centered and in control. Learn to find this state of mind on command.

AVOIDANCE OF EXCESS IN ALL THINGS is a natural spiritual law. Break it, and you will know why— disharmony will be close by.

Silence
breeds a mind
that knows no boundaries.

From a still mind the only boundaries are the ones you put there. From silence will come sensitivity and receptivity—from sensitivity and receptivity will come learning and awareness. From learning and awareness will come the ability to expand your boundaries.

There is an ancient saying: "Is the mind in the universe or is the universe within the mind?"

Where are the boundaries of time and space in your mind?

In essence, THERE ARE ONLY TWO THINGS IN THE UNIVERSE: YOU AND EVERYTHING ELSE! You are the only one of you in the universe. How do you relate with everything else?

All physical and spiritual laws are in relation to you and are what they are, because the laws simply work that way.

Stilling the mind is a very simple thing. But sometimes if the answer to a question is too simple, the mind has a tendency to think something is wrong. This is because your mind is too complex. Do not get distracted by complexity. Learn to simplify your life and complexity will be easier to see and handle.

Stillness of the mind will give you the clarity to see the answer, but are you ready to ask the question:

"Who am I?"

The green grass grows in the light
and is not seen in the darkness,
and while it is not seen,
does that mean it is not there?
And by whose eyes, seen and not seen?
Seeking light dispels darkness.
This is how growth appears.
Each time you gain insight into your life,
you gain insight
into why things are the way they are.
The insight about yourself is this light,
and this light dispels the darkness
of unknowing.
The problems in your life
hide in this darkness,
but does this mean the problems do not exist
if you are unaware of them?

It is only when you become aware of your problems that you can learn to work through them.

Each time you still your mind your light within brightens. The natural by-product of this light is understanding and the solutions to your problems.

Look to the light of understanding, and the darkness of unknowing will be a thing of the past, not a problem of the present. As you learn more about darkness you will understand it is not to be feared, but something to be learned from.

If you feel you are being plagued by a demon, you are being plagued by fear from within your own mind. It is the light of understanding that will illumine the "demons" of your mind. Cast light on the dark areas in your life and see for yourself that there are no demons—only the darkness of unknowing.

*The flowers blow in the wind
and the flowers are sometimes still,
much the same as your mind.
In time and on time,
all will grow to perfection.
But how was the journey
along the way?
One of many rocks or one of beauty?
You must decide,
many rocks or many flowers.*

In your life there will be times of great wind in your mind—the problems within your mind. There will also be times when your mind will be like a still mountain lake—when you are at peace with yourself. Between these two points are all of the ups and downs of life—the problems within you and the problems outside you. When it happens that the down side of life coincides with a time of great wind in your mind, much patience is needed. Control yourself and you will calm the storm.

When the winds of outside change are out of your control, know that you can take shelter in a calm mind. Create a calm shelter with the tools of self-control—practice concentration and meditation.

Everyone will stub their toe on rocks in their pathway from time to time. This is how we learn.

How many times will you stub your toe on the same rock?

The placement of your feet on your pathway is a determining factor. When you understand the factor, you will understand where you stand and why. Factor this!

*Weighing your life
is never an easy task,
that is why so many people avoid it.
To be truthful with one's self,
one must see the truth.*

There is no one more blind than someone who refuses to see. If you cannot see the truth, you will simply suffer. The truth is found in the way you use your mind to understand yourself. End the suffering through the illumination of your mind.

If you are afraid to weigh your life, you will always live in fear. Learn to trust yourself and understand your mind. Fear cannot exist in the light of awareness and understanding.

Learn to quiet your mind, so that you can see, hear, feel, sense and know what life is about.

When you have truthfully weighed your life, you will see that what you weigh is what you have within. Find love, beauty and happiness and your weight will be exactly right.

The weight of a feather is only heavy to those who cannot enjoy its beauty. The weight which you place upon yourself can be a feather or a brick.

Who decides which weight is assigned to each individual?

You
do not have to meditate,
but it would be wise to do so!

If I say to you, "You should meditate," you may not want to do it.

If you resent the fact that you are meditating, you will have difficulty or will not do it. Your own resentment will become a wall that will keep you from stilling your mind.

Meditation is a way to break down walls, not create new ones.

Meditate because you want to, not because you have to or because anybody says you should.

When you really understand what meditation does for your mind, you will meditate.

Give meditation some serious time and effort and if you continue to practice, one day down the line, you will know why it is wise to do so.

"*W*hen you are one
with yourself,
you will be
one with everything.
It is that simple!"

Chapter Nine
The Oneness of All

WACHTSTETTER

*Fondness of your fellow man
brings you to the understanding,
we are all one.
The separation comes in one's mind,
not in the color of your skin,
your religion or hair color.
The smallest separation is still a separation,
is it not?
The oneness you seek is not with all things
but with yourself.*

The destruction of mankind is a horrible thing.

How many times will a man kill another before he understands he is killing himself?

The bloodshed must stop within the individual. It will not come in groups or armies. When one is following one who does not know the truth, disaster is sure to follow. The pathway to truth is within your own mind, not in the world. The separation in the world is a result of a separation within each individual's own mind.

To understand yourself, you must wake up. When mankind wakes up out of the deep slumber of ignorance we will make great progress in the world. Wake up today! It is you who are separating yourself from the very thing you are looking for—oneness with yourself.

KINDNESS FOR YOUR FELLOW MAN IS VERY IMPORTANT. From kindness comes compassion, from compassion comes a more harmonious world. You can really do this—have kindness—but you must try with all your heart.

Is this not a noble cause for living and a beautiful way of being?

*W*hen you put your hands together
and feel yourself,
you will know you are one.

When you feel lost in the world, put your hands together and feel who you are. It is from the very simple practice of sitting down and communicating with yourself that you become acquainted with yourself.

Oh, it would be so easy if someone could just walk up to you and give you the essence of your life, but alas, it has never been done because it cannot. You must find it yourself. Find your spiritual presence in your practice not in outstretched hands to another. When your hands are full of well-being then it is time to reach out to another. Place your hands together and feel the presence deep within your soul. There are wonders awaiting you beyond your imagination.

The depth of your spirituality is in direct proportion to how much time you spend understanding yourself. Take time to put your hands together each day to feel and know more about yourself.

There is a profound understanding in the person that is you.

Within your own hands is your enlightenment. All you need do is seek it.

*He who separates himself,
separates himself from all that is.*

The surprise in life often comes to one who does not pay attention to the fine details in life. These details are usually the ones he does not wish to look at. When these details affect others, separation comes quickly. When the ball has begun to roll, oft times it is hard to control. When the point of reference is no control, there is only one direction to go—disharmony. When the strings of attachments have been pulled in close, you will see you need not hold onto them. When the individual can let go of disharmony, he can let people be.

If your religion or philosophy separates you from people, it is dogma and separates you from yourself and from everything that is spiritual. Separation is a lack of understanding that we are all one.

Fear, hate, prejudice, jealousy and resentment are weaknesses and need to be seen as such. These negative emotions are at the root of separation. Take time to find your weaknesses and get rid of them one by one.

True strength is in knowing yourself and making your life happy and content, but never at the expense of others. To obtain everything in life at the expense of others and have no one with which to share, can be a lonely and painful pathway that only leads one direction—unhappiness.

We have all come from one source and will one day return to it.

Why separate yourself from it?

*T*ake time
to look at the difference of culture,
but the sameness of people.

Whatever you are in life, you are of great importance. How important depends on you! Specialness depends not on hair color, color of skin or where you are from. When we are cut, we all bleed. When we are sad, we all cry and when we are happy, we are happy.

Are we all not the same within?

Learn to appreciate the difference in people. If we as people were all the same on the outside, life would be bland. Life would be without spice. Your individuality is your spice and your uniqueness. It is this that makes your life special.

It has been said in many ways, by many different teachers, from all parts of the world, we are all heading in the same direction: to GOD, PERFECTION, NIRVANA or MERGING WITH THE UNIVERSE. The separation is not in these terms but in the minds of people who do not understand them.

When you can see the big picture in life, you will see that your spirituality is of one true nature, a natural state of being. If you do not see yourself as part of nature, you will not understand your place in it. We may all look different but our essence is all the same.

*The difficulty
is not in the world
but in men's minds.*

The problems of the world are not going to be solved by something outside us. When we can solve the problems in our own lives, we will see clearly the problems of the world. It is the problems within people that create the problems of the world, not the reverse.

It is sad that mankind has to learn the hard way. But alas, it has been this way for a long time.

We must learn to teach by positive reinforcement, not negative action. From negative actions come negative results. Until teaching from a point of love becomes commonplace, mankind will continue to learn the hard way.

We must first care about ourselves before we can care about the world. Learning kindness, compassion, and love can happen in many ways. Find love in yourself, then pass it on to another; this will spark caring. What is learned is passed by example from one person to another. This is spiritual teaching at its finest.

If you try to help someone and they refuse your help, let them go. They may need to learn something that you cannot teach them. Some lessons in life are hard and that is all that can be said. If you are having difficulty in your life and cannot find the answers within, seek help from someone who has what you are looking for. All people need help from time to time.

Resolve the difficulty within your own mind and you will solve the difficulty in your world.

The making sense of the world is hard
when it is run by money and emotions.
Let us try to use rational thought,
the bridge to life itself.

When the emotions of people are out of control they can cause great havoc in the world. Rational thought is nowhere to be found when selfish emotions are riding high. When emotions are closer to animal than human, spirituality is hard to find.

Alas, many of the things that people look for in their lives are convoluted by their own minds. Rational thought in its present tense is a passing thing and not the stationary. There are no miracle cures to the world's problems; the only cure is within the mind of each individual.

Rational thought is the base from which you build a sound mind. When you are standing on your own foundation you may choose to build any way you wish. Your structure can be as elaborate as your mind can create or if you are lazy it may never be built at all. Between these two mediums is comfort.

When you have spent too much time attaining money, comfort within is hard to find—your inside world is lacking. When not working at all, comfort outside is hard to find—your outside world is lacking. Be comfortable in both worlds.

How much more could you ask for?

The gift
of the universe
is upon each
who seek its presence/presents.

The universe has a presence and presents to give. But you must be able to sense the presence and seek out the presents for yourself.

Seek and ye shall find! This is an ancient truth as are all truths. Truth is timeless and stands the test of time, because it works. If truth were anything else but the truth, it would not be truth. If truth is created from an individual's mind, it is not the truth. Truth is of a pure substance.

What more can be added to something that is already pure?

The presence of the universe has always been pure; it need not be created by a mind—it already is. When you recognize this fact you will recognize that you and the universe are of each other.

As you study and reach deep inside yourself you will find that everything in the universe is within you. Everything is already there; it has always been and always will be.

How could it be any other way?

You are part of it!

How much a part of it are you?

It is most wise to see reality the way it is.

Then it is not different.

How can you see the truth, if you change it?

It is not the truth.

That is the question, is it not?

Are you the truth?

Ponder the question of who you are.

It has great value!

Wise men have said it for eons.

Why do not more people believe it?

Perhaps, it is easier

to look outside to something else.

There are only three questions you need know the answers to in life:

Who are you?

Why are you here?

Where are you going?

It is hard to see who you are when you cannot see reality for what it is.

It is almost impossible to see the truth, if all you can do is see through preconceived ideas, prejudices and colored thoughts.

From your own clarity of mind will come the understanding of your spiritual pathway and the world around you. Learn to work with your mind to see what you can and cannot see. Remember, just because you cannot see something does not mean it is not there.

There are many things in the physical and spiritual universe that are seen and unseen. If you only see the physical universe, you are only seeing the physical part of it.

Still your mind and you will see the spiritual part of it.

*Learn to see truth
for what it is,
not because it came from someone.*

If you cannot see the truth in life for yourself, how do you know the philosophy, religion, or person you are following knows the truth?

The only way to truly know truth is through first hand experience—your experience!

Everyone must believe in something in life—believe in yourself.

You are the only person who can see the truth about who you are. This is why all spiritual masters throughout time have said to go within. All great spiritual teachers can only do one thing—point the way. It is you who must take the steps to find the truth for yourself. If you are not experiencing the truth of life from within, you are standing outside it.

The truth in life is a solitary experience. It does not come from a god. It comes from life.

The beauty
of your relationship
with God,
is that
it is created
by your thoughts,
from your own mind.

You were born an individual. You will live as an individual, and you will die as an individual.

What makes you think that you do not already have everything within you?

Your relationship with GOD or the UNIVERSE is one-to-one. All that is necessary is that you still your mind and learn to use all your senses, not just the physical ones.

Between what is pure and what is not is your life. It is from the appreciation of this pureness in life that produces beautiful thoughts on your walk toward GOD.

The more you understand the pureness within yourself, the more you will understand your relationship with GOD or the UNIVERSE.

It is as simple as that!

*The golden ring of completion
is given,
not by someone else,
but by you.*

We are all working on the completion of ourselves.

The feelings of satisfaction on your spiritual pathway come because of what you do, not because of what someone else does. You are the only one who can give yourself the satisfaction you seek.

When you have put all the pieces of your individual, personal, spiritual puzzle in place, and can move freely through life not interfering with anyone in any way, then. . . you will be an AVATAR—YOU WILL BE ABSOLUTE LOVE.

You will be absolute love because you will understand it is the most beautiful way to be.

The golden ring of completion is absolute love, not given by an angel of the Most High, but by the realization that you are that angel.

The last of the words
to be said
should be that
of coming together.

When we as individuals begin to recognize our imperfections and work to make ourselves complete beings, change in the world will come about smoothly. We will no longer see ourselves by our imperfections but as beings on a pathway to enlightenment.

Imperfections are nothing but the darkness of not understanding the pathway you walk in life.

The true pathway is one of understanding yourself.

We are all on a pathway to perfection; that perfection is GOD, the natural order of all things in the UNIVERSE.

When mankind realizes this as truth, the last of the words to be said will be those of coming together, first as individuals, and one day, as one people.

About the Author

The author began his formal studies in 1978 at a spiritual church in Encinitas, California. It was there that he met a teacher who taught meditation—stillness of the mind.

His studies included all Eastern and Western philosophies. In 1985 he became a licensed teacher and member of the staff. In February of 1990 he was ordained as a minister. In March of 1992 he went on a sabbatical to write this book.

Throughout Ron's life, he has spent a great deal of time seeking the answers to the many questions that he had—within. Through his personal experience he has found that when an individual is able to find harmony within, he can live a harmonious life.

Ron Rathbun is currently teaching meditation and spiritual philosophy in North San Diego County, California.